Essential English Swear Words

Stewart Ferris

summersdale

Copyright © Stewart Ferris 2004

All rights reserved. No part of this book may be reproduced by any means, nor transmitted, nor translated into a machine language, without the written permission of the publisher.

Summersdale Publishers Ltd
46 West Street
Chichester
PO19 1RP   UK

www.summersdale.com

ISBN 1 84024 418 6

Printed and bound in the EU.

Contents

Introduction..5

Swear words.......................................8

Top words for a man's front bottom...116

Top words for a lady's front bottom...117

Top words for a chocolate starfish....118

Top words for chutney ferrets...........119

Top words for bean flickers..............120

Top words for choking the chicken...121

Top words for notable jugs...............122

Introduction

People tell me swearing is offensive. But they can fuck off.

They tell me swearing is a sign of a weak vocabulary and a limited imagination. But they can go and ram it up their shitty arses.

Some even tell me it's not big and it's not clever. Would they still think that if I told them it was nine inches long and had a fucking degree in Media Studies?

There's a long and noble tradition of swear words in the English language, from Chaucer to Shakespeare and all the other boring bastards. So fucking what? Who cares about history? The only interesting thing about the history of swear words is that there used to be a street in London called Gropecunt Lane. Apparently. Then some tosser got the street renamed. Talk about political correctness gone mad.

Let's dispel a few myths here. Swearing makes you sound more grown up. It makes you sound hard, like the kind of rebel who wouldn't think twice about not disposing of his fast food packaging responsibly. The fact that swearing also happens to offend some people within earshot is just a bonus. Anyway, if they're offended it's their fault, not

INTRODUCTION

yours. If beauty is in the eye of the beholder, offensiveness is in the ear of the listener.

The only shame is that there are so few words around that have much shock value these days. You can't invent new swear words easily because people aren't offended by words that make no sense to them. Maybe the answer lies in the production of a suitable accompanying gesture to underline the meaning? But who cares? Just read the fucking tosspissing shitlicking book.

THE LITTLE BOOK OF ESSENTIAL ENGLISH SWEAR WORDS

"Arse"

ARSE

Definition:
A fat area of the body which is sat on, shat through and groped during slow dances. Often all in the same evening.

Usage:
'Arse!'
– generally applicable at times of disappointment, such as when your new girlfriend expresses keen interest in celibacy.

'My arse!'
– a fat TV Scouser's overused catchphrase.

'Does my arse look big in this?'
– to which the answer is 'Yes it does'.

ESSENTIAL ENGLISH SWEAR WORDS

THE LITTLE BOOK OF

"Arsehole"

ARSEHOLE

Definition:
Someone who demonstrates mental deficiency by pulling out in front of you in their car, spilling your pint in the pub, or voting Tory.

Usage:
'You're a complete arsehole'
– useful phrase for a plastic surgeon upon completion of anal reconstructive surgery.

'Don't be an arsehole all your life'
– try voting for a different party once in a while.

'This place is the arsehole of the earth'
– useful phrase if you're from Slough in Berkshire.

ESSENTIAL ENGLISH SWEAR WORDS

THE LITTLE BOOK OF

"Balls"

BALLS

Definition:
That of which Hitler only had one; squidgy things that tennis players hit during romp sessions; formal dances in which women wear low-cut gowns and men rub their nads against them whilst peering down their cleavage.

Usage:
'New balls please'
– Wimbledon umpire after prolonged sex.

'The ball was in!'
– scream of angry tennis player during sex with a capacious lady.

'What a load of balls'
– remark made by a visitor to a tennis ball factory.

THE LITTLE BOOK OF ESSENTIAL ENGLISH SWEAR WORDS

" Bastard "

BASTARD

Definition:
The bloke who nips into the parking space just before you; someone with a better-looking girlfriend than you; anyone who wins the lottery.

Usage:
'He's a right bastard!'
– a lottery winner who makes a valid point.

'Complete and utter bastard'
– someone who wins the lottery twice.

'A bit of a bastard'
– a gentleman who cheats on his lady and wins a quid on Lotto Instants.

ESSENTIAL ENGLISH SWEAR WORDS

THE LITTLE BOOK OF

"Beaver"

BEAVER

Definition:
Moist, furry mammal found in damp, dark places; to work very hard with the intention of gaining access to a moist, furry mammal.

Usage:
'What a fine beaver'
– what a fine moist, furry mammal.

'Can I stroke your beaver?'
– be careful that it doesn't bite your fingers off.

'Beaver away'
– probably downstream somewhere and working very hard.

ESSENTIAL ENGLISH SWEAR WORDS

THE LITTLE BOOK OF

" **Beef curtains** "

BEEF CURTAINS

Definition:
Meaty entrance to a lady's front bottom; hanging device to keep sunlight out of an abattoir.

Usage:

'Pull back those beef curtains so I can see if it's damp outside'
– phrase used by a butcher at work.

'Pull back those beef curtains so I can see if it's damp inside'
– phrase used by a butcher at home.

'Your beef curtains look like a double cheeseburger. Yum.'
– how not to flatter your lover.

'Your beef curtains look like a double cheeseburger with ketchup. Yum.'
– how not to flatter your lover during rag week.

ESSENTIAL ENGLISH SWEAR WORDS

THE LITTLE BOOK OF

"**Bitch**"

BITCH

Definition:
A woman who won't sleep with you even though you bought her a pint (maybe you should have stretched to something with alcohol in it?); a female dog (who won't sleep with you either).

Usage:
'You're a stupid bitch!'
– a woman (or dog) who won't sleep with you who has an IQ of less than 90.

'Do the washing up, bitch'
– correct way to request the cleaning of the dishes.

'Nibble on my cock, bitch'
– instruction to a woman (or dog) who won't sleep with you to eat the chicken dinner you've lovingly prepared.

ESSENTIAL ENGLISH SWEAR WORDS

THE LITTLE BOOK OF

"Bloody"

BLOODY

Definition:
Contraction of 'by our lady' (a 15th century curse against Lady Thatcher); general adjective used to make the speaker sound moderately hard; the state of a jam rag at the end of its shift.

Usage:
'Oh bloody hell'
– it's not rag week again, is it?

'It's not bloody fair'
– rag week has dragged on for ten days and you're choking for a bit of action.

'Yuch! It's all bloody'
– after you've given up waiting.

ESSENTIAL ENGLISH SWEAR WORDS

THE LITTLE BOOK OF

"Bollocks"

BOLLOCKS

Definition:
Exclamation made when a potent fart is traced back to you; accusation of lying after you blame your bottom burp on the dog; a sperm factory kept between a gentleman's legs.

Usage:
'Oh bollocks!'
– when your sister's caught you choking your chicken in her underwear drawer.

'You're talking a load of bollocks!'
– when you try to deny your sister's story in front of the rest of the family.

'Bollocking bollocks that hurt!'
– when your sister's boyfriend tries to teach you a lesson in morality.

ESSENTIAL ENGLISH SWEAR WORDS

THE LITTLE BOOK OF

"**Bugger**"

BUGGER

Definition:
The insertion of a trouser truncheon into a Gary Glitter; insult applicable to lawyers; exclamation of disappointment when your lawyer's bill is huge despite the favours you did to him that resulted in you waddling like a duck for a week.

Usage:
'I want to bugger you'
– I am a lawyer

'You little bugger!'
– why won't you let me bugger you?

'Oh bugger'
– I didn't realise you were an undercover policeman.

ESSENTIAL ENGLISH SWEAR WORDS

THE LITTLE BOOK OF

> "**Bum bandit**"

BUM BANDIT

Definition:
Mexican outlaw in a large, colourful hat who rather pointlessly specialises in robbing homeless people; affectionate term for a shirt lifter.

Usage:
'Are you calling me a bum bandit?'
– does the swag sack full of bums give me away or is it the hat?

'You bum bandit!'
– give me back my wallet, my handbag and my arse.

'That moustache makes you look like a bum bandit'
– a phrase that was inexplicably never used by any of Hitler's senior generals.

ESSENTIAL ENGLISH SWEAR WORDS

THE LITTLE BOOK OF

"Carpet muncher"

CARPET MUNCHER

Definition:
One who dines on *tarte au poile*; a tuppence licker; a muff diver; a very hungry person in a carpet shop.

Usage:
'Oi, let go, you carpet muncher!'
– exclamation of an angry carpet shop assistant when a customer attaches his boat race to her beaver.

'She looks like a carpet muncher'
– useful descriptive phrase when spotting a butch-looking woman with wool threads hanging from the corners of her mouth.

'Get me the head carpet muncher!'
– probably the least useful phrase in the English language.

ESSENTIAL ENGLISH SWEAR WORDS

THE LITTLE BOOK OF

"Cock"

COCK

Definition:
The rancid-looking husband of a chicken; adjective applicable to any annoying person; that which needs to be sucked by a cocksucker.

Usage:
'Suck my cock'
– chat-up line for those who like to try the direct approach.

'Oh go on, please suck my cock – I washed it last week especially'
– backup line for when the direct approach inevitably fails.

'Careful, doctor – that's where she hit me when I asked her to suck my cock'
– useful medical phrase.

ESSENTIAL ENGLISH SWEAR WORDS

THE LITTLE BOOK OF

"Cocksucker"

COCKSUCKER

Definition:
One who loiters around a poultry farm with a straw; a shitty or unpopular person; the kind of girlfriend all blokes aspire to obtain.

Usage:
'Oi, cocksucker, get orrf moi laaand!'
– poultry farmer's exclamation of anger to the freak with the big straw.

'You're such a big cocksucker'
– huge compliment to a girl
and a big insult to a chap.

'Are you a cocksucker?
If so, how often?'
– when interviewing a potential girlfriend.

ESSENTIAL ENGLISH SWEAR WORDS

THE LITTLE BOOK OF

"Crap"

CRAP

Definition:
An old computer; all teams other than the one you support; your chances of getting on in life with this kind of vocabulary; a crap card game; a plop.

Usage:
'Your sexual technique is crap'
– not surprising considering you've only practiced on your own.

'I need to take a crap'
– leave it there, don't take it with you unless you're walking the dog in which case make sure it clears up the mess after you.

'Why is my computer so crap?'
– because its processor is busy wanking over all the porn you've downloaded.

ESSENTIAL ENGLISH SWEAR WORDS

THE LITTLE BOOK OF

> "**Cunt**"

CUNT

Definition:
Versatile word that describes literally *any* annoying person on the telly; someone who gets better exam results than you; a pleasant word for the female minge area
(girls love to hear this word . . . try it!).

Usage:
'I've just seen that cunt off the telly'
– Jeremy XXXXXXXX (name obscured for legal reasons and because he's a cunt).

'No, I meant that other cunt off the telly'
– Michael XXXXXXX (name obscured for legal reasons and because he's also a cunt).

'I think I've just seen your cunt'
– telephone call to the BBC to let them know that one of their cunts just winked at you in the street.

ESSENTIAL ENGLISH SWEAR WORDS

THE LITTLE BOOK OF

"Dickhead"

DICKHEAD

Definition:
A person who drives the wrong way down a one-way street; someone who loudly proclaims unsubstantiated opinions; the shiny end of a pink trouser sausage.

Usage:
'You're a dickhead'
– if you were going to talk to the parts of your own body this might be a good place to start.

'Keep your dickhead opinions to yourself'
– please stop telling me your thoughts about the shiny end of your pink trouser sausage.

'Sorry Officer, I'm just a dickhead'
– your excuse for being caught driving the wrong way down a one way street.

ESSENTIAL ENGLISH SWEAR WORDS

THE LITTLE BOOK OF

> **Div**

Definition:
The kid at school with any minor physical imperfection which it would be polite to ignore but more fun to emphasise by calling him a div even though it's going to fuck up his personality for 20 years and could turn him into a sadistic dictator.

Usage:
'Hey, Adolf, you divvy one nad'
– the reason World War Two started.

'Hey Saddam, you're such a div with that dead rat under your nose'
– the reason the Gulf War started.

'Hey George, you're a total divvy shit'
– I bet that kid is regretting his words now.

ESSENTIAL ENGLISH SWEAR WORDS

THE LITTLE BOOK OF

"**Felch**"

FELCH

Definition:
An unfortunately named town; an unfortunate surname; removal by oral means of a gentleman's mayonnaise from the chocolate starfish of another.

Usage:
'Taxi driver – I'm going to Felch'
– make sure you have enough tissues to clean the back of the cab afterwards.

'Have you been felching again or is that ice cream on your face?'
– it's very hard to tell when it's vanilla flavour.

'Are you felching me or have you just stuck a sardine up my arse?'
– to which you reply 'Just keep your eye on the road, taxi driver'.

ESSENTIAL ENGLISH SWEAR WORDS

THE LITTLE BOOK OF

> **Fuck**

FUCK

Definition:
Shag; expression of disappointment when you realise through your drunken stupor that not only has the condom split but she's also your cousin.

Usage:
'Fancy a fuck?'
– a romantic chat-up line with guaranteed results (a kick in the goolies).

'Fuck: my husband's home early. Get into the wardrobe'
– make the most of it by trying on her underwear for the next two hours while her husband unwittingly helps himself to sloppy seconds.

'Fuck this for a game of soldiers'
– when you've tried on all her underwear and decide to give up hiding and go home.

ESSENTIAL ENGLISH SWEAR WORDS

THE LITTLE BOOK OF

> **Fuck all**

FUCK ALL

Definition:
Given the option of banging a selection of rancid whores, you drunkenly decide to take the lot; a situation in which none of the range of options pleases you, such as when you're sober enough to realise how rancid all the whores are.

Usage:
'You've got fuck all between your ears'
– well let's hope she doesn't mind that you've got fuck all between your legs.

'I've got fuck all money'
– it would have been easier to say 'I've got no money' and would actually have increased your chances of getting a job in order to earn some.

'There's fuck all to do in this town'
– well get a bus out of Slough, then.

THE LITTLE BOOK OF ESSENTIAL ENGLISH SWEAR WORDS

> **Fuck off**

FUCK OFF

Definition:
A request for an annoying cunt to leave your vicinity; an expression of disbelief such as when you're told it's your turn to wash up.

Usage:
'Fuck off!'
– I don't want to lose my anal virginity tonight.

'Fuck off!'
– please remove yourself from my vicinity forthwith, you annoying cunt.

'Fuck off!'
– how can you declare a No Fly Zone around your twat so soon after the last one ended? Has it really been three weeks?

ESSENTIAL ENGLISH SWEAR WORDS

THE LITTLE BOOK OF

"Fucked"

FUCKED

Definition:
The final declaration that something is broken despite your attempts to repair it by hitting it and kicking it; the moment when all hope is lost, such as when England goes into a penalty shoot-out; the grateful bit of flange in your bed.

Usage:
'You're well and truly fucked'
– useful phrase for an accident and emergency ward doctor to a well mashed patient at work.

'I'm all fucked up because I'm rich'
– a hoit's legal defence against drug charges.

'You're well and truly fucked'
– useful phrase for an accident and emergency ward doctor to a well mashed bird at home.

ESSENTIAL ENGLISH SWEAR WORDS

THE LITTLE BOOK OF

"Fuckity-fuck"

FUCKITY-FUCK

Definition:
Expression of disappointment when the exotic girl you drunkenly lured into your hotel bed in Thailand turns out to be a boy but you're too pissed to let that get in the way of the hot romp your bollocks have been aching for.

Usage:
'Oh fuckity fuck'
– my mates warned me about people like you but I thought they were kidding. Still, you look like a bird from behind and that's enough for me.

'Oh fuckity fuck'
– I didn't want you to do *that* to me. Ouch!

'Oh fuckity fuck'
– honestly darling, I accidentally sat on a bathtap in my Bangkok hotel on that business trip, that's why it's so sore.

THE LITTLE BOOK OF ESSENTIAL ENGLISH SWEAR WORDS

" **God** "

GOD

Definition:
One who created everything and therefore takes credit for all that is good and bad, and who by fairly tenuous logic is also responsible for the creation of all swear words and the joy they bring to so many people; the word most commonly uttered at the moment of orgasm; 'dog' spelled backwards.

Usage:
'Oh God, oh God, oh Gooooodddddd!'
– typical utterance at the moment of creation (of a baby).

'My God, you're such a fucking blasphemer'
– typical utterance of a bishop with an actress at the moment of orgasm.

ESSENTIAL ENGLISH SWEAR WORDS

THE LITTLE BOOK OF

"Jam rag"

JAM RAG

Definition:
Mouse-like roll of cotton wool that birds stuff up their bacon sandwiches to ensure you can't insert your love truncheon while the decorators are busy painting the town red.

Usage:
'Time to change the guards at Buckingham Palace – I need a jam rag'
– request for a assistance when caught short.

'Too late – they're already trooping the colour. Forget jam rags, pass me a mop'
– the consequences of not putting jam rags in your handbag.

'A packet of jam rags, please – Niagra Falls strength'
– how to ask for them in the chemist's.

ESSENTIAL ENGLISH SWEAR WORDS

THE LITTLE BOOK OF

"**Jesus Christ**"

JESUS CHRIST

Definition:
Exclamation of shock at the size of someone's jugs; Essene-Judaic prophet born around the time of Christ who invented Christmas.

Usage:
'Jesus Christ!'
– I've never seen jugs large enough to have their own gravitational pull before.

'Jesus H. Christ!'
– what did you hit me for? I was only looking at them, for fuck's sake.

'Jesus H. mud jousting Christ!'
– stop hitting me! Anyway, with jugs that big how can I not look at them?

ESSENTIAL ENGLISH SWEAR WORDS

THE LITTLE BOOK OF

> **Joey**

JOEY

Definition:
One who makes a simple mistake; one who can't get their words out; a religious minister who makes a simple mistake, especially a Deacon.

Usage:
'Don't be such a Joey'
– don't be such a spazzmo.

'What do you mean, you don't know what I mean by Joey?'
– don't be such a div.

'Joey! You know? Joooeeey!'
– you realise this insult shows your age because no one under 30 remembers the *Blue Peter* reports you're referring to.

ESSENTIAL ENGLISH SWEAR WORDS

THE LITTLE BOOK OF

" Jugs "

JUGS

Definition:
Receptacles for carrying beer; mammalian frontal stereo appendage evolved for the purpose of providing images for magazine centrefolds; a reason for living.

Usage:
'Nice jugs. Can I lick them?'
– nice try, but probably won't work.

'Nice jugs. Can I photograph them?'
– a better option, as you can always lick the photo later.

'Nice jugs. How much?'
– a polite enquiry to a frontally endowed homewares assistant.

ESSENTIAL ENGLISH SWEAR WORDS

THE LITTLE BOOK OF

"Motherfucker"

MOTHERFUCKER

Definition:
Insult of American origin referring to any displeasing person of American origin; one who indulges in rumpy-pumpy with their mother; hilarious rock 'n' roll slang for humbucker guitar pickups; something that won't work.

Usage:
'You motherfucker!'
– not only have you displeased me in some way but I also have reason to believe that you may be American in ethnicity.

'Why won't this motherfucker start?'
– you're not hitting it with a big enough hammer.

'My axe has two motherfuckers'
– what a sad motherfucker.

ESSENTIAL ENGLISH SWEAR WORDS

THE LITTLE BOOK OF

> **Mud Jouster**

MUD JOUSTER

Definition:
One whose preferred route for the delivery of pleasure is the Hershey Highway; one who packs brown, dairy and sugar-based confectionery in a Devon factory for a living; one who finds mud on the end of his lance after same-sex shenanigans.

Usage:
'You can tell he's a mud jouster.'
'How?'
'Look at his drink – it's a half pint.'

'You can tell he's a mud jouster.'
'How?'
'Look at the way he stands.'

'You can tell he's a mud jouster.'
'How?'
'Look at the shit on the end of his cock.'

ESSENTIAL ENGLISH SWEAR WORDS

THE LITTLE BOOK OF

"Pearl necklace"

PEARL NECKLACE

Definition:
String of pearls worn around stuck-up necks of rich hoity-toity birds; the visual effect of a string of pearls worn around the grubby neck of some slapper you've just shot your load all over.

Usage:
'Darling, I want a pearl necklace'
– time to remove your trousers.

'No, put it away, I want a *real* pearl necklace!'
– stuck up cow: who does she think she is?

'Is that a pearl necklace or did you spill some Tippex down your neck?'
– the best way to tell is to get up close to her neck and sniff. She won't mind.

ESSENTIAL ENGLISH SWEAR WORDS

THE LITTLE BOOK OF

" Piss "

PISS

Definition:
Weak lager that looks and tastes the same when it enters the body as when it leaves; strange wet patches that appear in doorways after 11pm on Saturday nights; unexplained discolouration on your trousers on Sunday mornings.

Usage:
'This wine tastes of piss'
– useful phrase for a restaurant critic.

'I won't take the piss out of this beer, otherwise there'll be nothing left'
– useful phrase for a pissy beer critic.

'It's not piss on my trousers. It's wine.'
– useful excuse for a restaurant critic on a Sunday morning.

THE LITTLE BOOK OF ESSENTIAL ENGLISH SWEAR WORDS

"Pissed"

PISSED

Definition:
A state of inebriation also known as 'beer goggles' which can transform an ugly boiler into a borderline beauty; a state of having just emptied your bladder onto a sleeping American Inter-Railer; an annoyed American.

Usage:
'I'm so pissed'
– I'll put my lunch box in your trout mouth even though you look like a failed medical experiment.

'I pissed myself laughing'
– it's time to grow out of knock-knock jokes.

'I'm very angry and pissed'
– you shouldn't have gone to sleep with your mouth open when you've got a face like a urinal and the stars and stripes on your rucksack.

ESSENTIAL ENGLISH SWEAR WORDS

THE LITTLE BOOK OF

"Piss off"

PISS OFF

Definition:
To make someone angry by stealing their chips; instruction to a chip thief to go away and never return; expression of disbelief that anyone would have the audacity to steal your chips.

Usage:
'Piss off!'
– typical response to a chat-up line.

'Look, she told you to piss off. Which part of 'piss off' don't you understand?'
– you'll understand all of it with this handy book!

'He said *what* to you? Piss off!'
– her friend can't believe that you tried to chat her up by saying you were no longer infected.

ESSENTIAL ENGLISH SWEAR WORDS

THE LITTLE BOOK OF

" Prick "

PRICK

Definition:
A minor sensation of irritating pain that a woman feels when one is inserted into her; someone who wears sunglasses indoors in order to keep a low profile but who actually stands out a mile; a small serving of pork sword.

Usage:
'You may feel a little prick but it's nothing to be scared of'
– useful phrase for a doctor when giving permission for a patient to delve into his trousers.

'You big prick'
– flattery if the recipient is naked or abuse if he's dressed.

'Did you just prick me?'
– never a flattering question.

ESSENTIAL ENGLISH SWEAR WORDS

THE LITTLE BOOK OF

> **Pussy**

PUSSY

Definition:
The most famous part of Mrs Slocombe's anatomy; favourite porn world term for a lady's front bottom; affectionate term for a pet cat.

Usage:
'My pussy loves the taste of fish'
– Mrs Slocombe in the fish shop.

'Can you feel my pussy in there?'
– when the vet can't see Mrs Slocombe's cat in its travel box.

'My pussy likes to be tickled'
– Mrs Slocombe in bed with her cat.

THE LITTLE BOOK OF ESSENTIAL ENGLISH SWEAR WORDS

"**Quim**"

QUIM

Definition:
The heavily guarded entrance to a lady's love tunnel; protected Brazilian rain forest; minge.

Usage:
'Doctor, I think there's something living deep in my quim'
– useful medical phrase.

'I'd like a quim trim please'
– useful phrase when visiting the hairdressers on the doctor's recommendation.

'If I give you a Brazilian wax on that quim it could undermine the El Niño weather system'
– oh dear, you've left it too late.

THE LITTLE BOOK OF ESSENTIAL ENGLISH SWEAR WORDS

"Shag"

SHAG

Definition:
A brand of pouch tobacco; a stupidly named dance; a type of fluffy carpet; oh, and the act of fornication.

Usage:
'Fancy a shag?'
– chat-up line involving the proffering of one's pouch and a lighter.

'Fancy a deep shag?'
– used by carpet sales assistants to determine a customer's sexual preferences

'I really enjoyed that shag'
– used by a man with a roll-up in his mouth after a dance on a fluffy carpet followed by a damn good rogering.

ESSENTIAL ENGLISH SWEAR WORDS

THE LITTLE BOOK OF

"**Shit**"

SHIT

Definition:
That which is excreted from the mouth of a liar; that which is excreted from the arse; a word to describe someone's performance in bed where the other person is left feeling like they've only had a rehearsal; that which a rabbit considers to be a wholesome meal.

Usage:
'You're shit in the sack'
– well let's try it on a bed like everyone else.

'Yuch! Is that shit on your fingers?'
– well stop licking them, then.

'You talk a lot of shit'
– I have to because I sell manure for a living.

ESSENTIAL ENGLISH SWEAR WORDS

THE LITTLE BOOK OF

> "**Shit creek**"

SHIT CREEK

Definition:
Generic word describing all Australian wines; a metaphorical dead end; amusing term for an Australian's anus.

Usage:
'We're up shit creek without a paddle'
– crappy Australian cliché meaning our wine tastes like piss so the only people dumb enough to buy will be the Brits.

'I think I'm up shit creek'
– typically Australian response to the question 'Are you sure it's in the right hole?'

'This is a shit creek'
– Australian Professor of Medicine explaining the parts of the body to new students.

ESSENTIAL ENGLISH SWEAR WORDS

THE LITTLE BOOK OF

"Shithead"

SHITHEAD

Definition:
The lead end of a turd (usually less pointy than the tail in case you were wondering how to identify it, but a more worrying question is why would you want to identify it in the first place?); a despicable person who has faecal deposits where the brain should be.

Usage:
'You're a fucking cocksucking arsefelching shithead'
– term of endearment in the north of England.

'You shithead!'
– you despicable person who seems to have faecal deposits where the brain should be.

'Is that the shithead?
It looks too pointy'
– who cares?

ESSENTIAL ENGLISH SWEAR WORDS

THE LITTLE BOOK OF

> "Shit Stabber"

SHIT STABBER

Definition:
Amateur murderer who lacks proficiency with his knife; employee of a sewage treatment plant who pokes blockages with a long stick; one who uses the tradesmen's entrance even when the front door's open.

Usage:
'You're a shit stabber'
– don't stab me in the leg, go for the chest.

'I always dreamed of being a shit stabber when I was a little boy'
– useful phrase when being interviewed for a job at the sewage treatment plant.

'I'm a shit stabber so roll over'
– I don't want to get mud on your carpet so I'll go round the back.

ESSENTIAL ENGLISH SWEAR WORDS

THE LITTLE BOOK OF

"Snatch"

SNATCH

Definition:
The part of Madonna that inspired Guy Ritchie's greatest film; to steal a Guy Ritchie DVD from boxing promoters and jewellers; a neat and tidy quim.

Usage:
'I'd like to see your Snatch –
I've heard so much about it'
– Madonna's chat-up line to Guy Ritchie

'I'd like to see your Snatch –
I've heard so much about it'
– Guy Ritchie's chat-up line to Madonna

'Don't snatch at it'
– Madonna and Guy Ritchie
in bed with his DVDs.

ESSENTIAL ENGLISH SWEAR WORDS

THE LITTLE BOOK OF

"Sodding"

SODDING

Definition:
General disparaging adjective that can be prefixed to any politician's name; the addition of a layer of soil to the ground; the process of dropping anchor in Poo Bay.

Usage:
'Get off my sodding lawn!'
– please refrain from walking on the soil I've just laid on my lawn.

'You're a sodding liar!'
– I am hotly disputing your claim to have laid soil on my lawn.

'Wipe that sodding smile off your face'
– restore your facial muscles to the position they were in before you dropped anchor in Poo Bay.

ESSENTIAL ENGLISH SWEAR WORDS

THE LITTLE BOOK OF

> **Sod off**

SOD OFF

Definition:
Instruction for someone who desires to navigate your windward passage to vacate your presence forthwith; the result of loose topsoil and strong winds.

Usage:
'Sod off'
– initial typical response to a lad's chat-up line.
Keep trying, though.

'Look, I said sod off, OK?'
– you know she doesn't mean it.
It has to be worth one more go.

'Why don't you just sod off
and leave me alone?'
– you're in there, mate!

ESSENTIAL ENGLISH SWEAR WORDS

THE LITTLE BOOK OF

"Slag"

SLAG

Definition:
A by-product of the steel-making process used in concrete mixes that is environmentally sound, is a renewable resource, and will sleep with anyone.

Usage:
'You slag!'
– you by-product of the steel-making process used in concrete mixes that is environmentally sound, is a renewable resource, and will sleep with anyone.

'Don't slag her off'
– refrain from casting aspersions about her integrity, her honour, and whether her arse is visible from space.

'On the slag heap'
– an optional extra at a brothel, involving a pile of three wanton sacks of concrete mix.

ESSENTIAL ENGLISH SWEAR WORDS

THE LITTLE BOOK OF

"Spunk"

SPUNK

Definition:
Australian term for a good looking boy;
American term for bravery;
British term for sex wee.

Usage:
'Look at that spunky spunk!'
– Australian girl on seeing a British boy after he has played pocket billiards without a tissue.

'How come I'm always
lying in the spunk?'
– moan from an ungrateful girlfriend in bed.

'He's full of spunk'
– American girl on seeing a brave
boy with nuts ready to burst.

THE LITTLE BOOK OF ESSENTIAL ENGLISH SWEAR WORDS

"Tits"

TITS

Definition:
A variety of bird found in the garden (in the jaws of the cat); people who wear bow ties; people who get excited about art (except art with tits in it); the contents of the top half of a bikini.

Usage:
'Tits out for the lads!'
– phrase used by male ornithologists keen to see some tits.

'It's all gone tits-up'
– when a well-endowed woman slips on a banana skin.

'Stop making a tit of yourself'
– take that bow tie off.

ESSENTIAL ENGLISH SWEAR WORDS

THE LITTLE BOOK OF

"Tosser"

TOSSER

Definition:
One who throws cabers, wellies and other pointless things; a proponent of solo hand sports; a shitty fascist with no sense of humour (such as the teacher who confiscated this book from you).

Usage:
'I am a tosser'
– proud boast of an Olympic wellie thrower in relation to his work.

'I am a tosser'
– proud boast of an Olympic wellie thrower in relation to his sex life.

'Don't be such a tosser'
– OK, you've had a childish laugh in the staff room with the other fascist teachers, now give this book back to the kid you confiscated it from.

ESSENTIAL ENGLISH SWEAR WORDS

THE LITTLE BOOK OF

> **Turd burglar**

TURD BURGLAR

Definition:
Retarded raider who illegally removes faecal deposits; the foreign burglar behind the first and the second burglars; an employee of a gentleman's clothing shop with responsibility for placing the shirts on a higher shelf.

Usage:
'Get out of my pants you turd burglar!'
– useful phrase if an unwanted burglar tries to follow the example of the first two burglars who entered your pants with permission.

'You're da turd burglar dis morning'
– frustrated foreigner who keeps getting violated.

'He looks like a turd burglar'
– referring to a retarded masked raider covered in shit seen emerging from a manhole.

ESSENTIAL ENGLISH SWEAR WORDS

THE LITTLE BOOK OF

> **Twat**

TWAT

Definition:
Someone who gets an erection just from listening to Mozart (his music, not his voice on a kinky classical music sex hotline); a woman's area on which a chap or a bean flicker can enjoy a fish supper.

Usage:
'What a twat!'
– appropriate thing to say to someone who trips over and is hurt in a relatively minor way.

'Were you always an arsehole and a twat, or were you once just a twat?'
– appropriate thing to say to someone who restarts the pub jukebox to replace your song with their favourite Val Doonican hit.

'What a twat!'
– appropriate thing to say when presented with a bush that is in urgent need of topiary.

ESSENTIAL ENGLISH SWEAR WORDS

"Wanker"

THE LITTLE BOOK OF

WANKER

Definition:
Anyone who drives a better car than you; someone who likes to indulge in a hand shandy; a person you dislike enough to whisper abuse at when you're sure they're out of earshot.

Usage:
'You wanker!'
– your actions indicate to me that there is a high probability that you are a spanker of apes.

'How dare you call me a wanker?'
– does my right arm really look that much more developed than my left?

'Look at that rich wanker'
– you have an automatic right to abuse someone who works hard for their money while you sit on your arse reading books of rude words.

ESSENTIAL ENGLISH SWEAR WORDS

THE LITTLE BOOK OF

"**Whore**"

WHORE

Definition:
A woman who won't ride your single barrel pump action shotgun unless you pay even though she should pay you for the privilege; general abusive term for rancid tarts who look like they carry more diseases than a hospital ward.

Usage:
'You're a whore?'
– why didn't you tell me this before we got married? How am I supposed to pay for the last 300 nights I spent rogering you?

'Great, you're a whore!'
– I won't have to pretend to be charming, or take you to dinner or even wash my honourable member for Pantington.

'She looks like a whore'
– try not to sound too excited when you say this.

ESSENTIAL ENGLISH SWEAR WORDS

Top words for a man's front bottom

Nob
Dick
Willy
Lunch box
One eyed trouser snake
Single barrel pump action shotgun
Love truncheon
Pork sword
The honourable member for Pantington
John Thomas
Pant python
Sex serpent
Pink oboe
Purple poker
Meat missile
Third leg

Top words for a lady's front bottom

Minge
Twat
Snatch
Fur burger
Sperm receptacle
Muff
Bacon sandwich
Trout mouth
Piss flaps
Hair pie
Black forest gateau
Brazilian rain forest
Quim
Plenge
Love tunnel
Fish supper
Protected area of outstanding natural beauty

THE LITTLE BOOK OF ESSENTIAL ENGLISH SWEAR WORDS

Top words for a chocolate starfish

Shit creek
Hershey highway
Chocolate factory
Marmite machine
Fudge department
Gary Glitter
Brown eye
Back alley

Top words for chutney ferrets

Arse bandit
Shit stabber
Fudge packer
Shirt lifter
Rear gunner
Cocoa shunter
Uphill gardener
Nob jockey
Rear admiral
Batty boy
Lord of the ring
Marmite masher
Navigator of the windward passage

ESSENTIAL ENGLISH SWEAR WORDS

Top words for bean flickers

Tuppence licker
Muff diver
Carpet muncher
Rug muncher
Clit hopper
Dyke
Dutch girl
Beef curtain pullers
Lezzers
Muff buffers
Fanny scratchers
Fish sniffers

Top words for choking the chicken

Spanking the monkey
Hand shandy
Thomas tank
Trouser snooker
Shaking hands with the unemployed
Rifle practice
Wanking
Jerking off
Five finger shuffle
Merchant bank
Switching to manual
Making your third eye cry
Sex with someone you love
Three shakes more than a piss

ESSENTIAL ENGLISH SWEAR WORDS

Top words for notable jugs

Norks
Bristols
Wabs
Melons
Thr'penny bits
Dumplings
Air bags
Udders
Pneumatic chest
Knockers
Bazookas
Gunzagas
Babylons
Tats

ALSO FROM SUMMERSDALE

SEXY FRENCH
- getting it on in France
All the French phrases you'll ever need for flirting with a Frenchie, getting them into bed, and telling the doctor the next morning that it now hurts when you wee.

ALSO FROM SUMMERSDALE

THE LITTLE BOOK OF
**ESSENTIAL
FOREIGN SWEAR WORDS**

When you go abroad, it's useful to know whether the policeman shoving his truncheon up your arse is calling you a bastard or a cunt. This book has all the words they forgot to mention at school.

ALSO FROM SUMMERSDALE

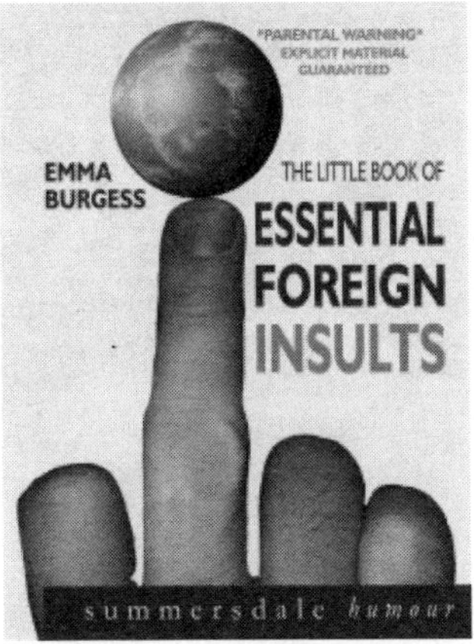

THE LITTLE BOOK OF
ESSENTIAL FOREIGN INSULTS

Communicating your superior opinions to Johnny Foreigner can be an uphill struggle at the best of times, but with this essential phrase book you can indulge in derogatory discourse wherever you travel and make sure they get the message.

ALSO FROM SUMMERSDALE

THE LITTLE BOOK OF
CHAT-UP LINES
This is the pocket collection of all the most hilarious chat-up lines and devastating put downs ever uttered.

ALSO FROM SUMMERSDALE

THE LITTLE BOOK OF
DIRTY JOKES

Like children playing in the mud, we all like a bit of filth! A collection of new and the classic lairy laughs.

- Hundreds of Summersdale books

- Free sample chapters

www.summersdale.com

- Author information

- New title previews